Intro to Red Deer Hunting

For Kids

Frank W Koretum

Table of Content

Red Deer Hunting 1
History of Red Deer 2
History 6
Red Deer in the United States 10
Red Deer Build 12
Knowing Your Gear 15
Guns and Scopes 16
Shotguns 17
Rifles 21
Arrows and Bows 24
Bowhunting Tips 26
Safety 27
Deer Stands 28
Deer Stand Safety 31
Deer Scents 34
Scouting 37
Tracking 39
Aiming 42
Field Dressings 43
General Safety 45
Food to Pack 47
Sandwiches 48
Beef Jerky 49
Soft Granola and Nutrition Bars 50
Understanding Conservation 51
Recap 55

Red Deer Hunting

Your blood runs cold for a split second as you spot the massive animal feet below your stand, high up in the trees. You have to look it over – is that a deer or an elk? You run through the list in your mind, checking off the signs. That's a Red Deer. You turn off the safety on your gun, take a deep breath, and aim….

History of Red Deer

Shortly after Europeans arrived in the New World, they met a creature that looked a lot like a bigger version of the red deer they had back home. However, it sounded very different, making a high, wild whistle instead of the deep roar of the red deer.

They gave the animal the name "Elk," and since then, people have argued about what it is. The main question was if elk are a subspecies of red deer or not. But in 2004, a mitochondrial DNA test proved for sure that red deer and elk are two different species.

Looking back, there are also many ways in which the two are different. Elk cows carry their babies for 20 days longer than red deer do, and bull elk carry their antlers for 35 days longer than red deer stags. Elk give birth after 255 days, while red deer give birth after 235 days.

Also, a bull elk weighs an average of 720 pounds, while a male red deer weighs only 400 pounds on average. And, of course, hearing an elk bugle is very different from hearing a red deer roar. There's a lot of similarities, that's true, but there are also a lot of differences!

History

The American Indian way of life in North America initially included a significant amount of deer hunting. The "venison" from a large deer could feed many tribal members with one kill, even. This is shown by the fact that Native Americans used bones and skin to make tools and clothing – if there was enough bone material and skin, also known as hide, we can safely make an educated guess there was plenty enough meat.

When Europeans first arrived in North America in the 1500s, American Indians began exchanging deerskins with the newcomers for tools and supplies. There were around 5 million deer hunted annually at the height of the deerskin trade.

Only around 500,000 white-tailed deer, the most common, remained in North America by the late 1800s. State and federal restrictions began to be implemented around the turn of the 20th century to preserve the declining herds of deer. Hunters found it more difficult to sell unlawfully slaughtered wild animals after the Lacy Act of 1900. Deer numbers rapidly began to increase once again.

Today, North America is home to more than 20 million deer. Hunting deer has become a popular hobby. Hunters still like to eat the deer they kill. But it's also important to enjoy the hunt and spend time in nature. Many hunters pass down the family tradition of hunting deer from one generation to the next.

Red Deer in the United States

When we talk about the Red Deer, which is actually more common in Europe and the U.K., some ranches in the United States have begun breeding programs and ranges for Red Deer due to the fact that they are big and offer a hunter some challenge without being as dangerous as Elk.

Strangely enough, some hunters have even reported seeing Red Deer in other places like the woods of Georgia, far away from any recognized breeding programs. Have a few escaped deer started a whole new population? Wildlife experts aren't quite sure yet!

Red Deer Build

The Red Deer is the biggest deer in the U.K., where they are from. The males have big, branching antlers that get bigger as they age. During the "rut," which is the fall breeding season, males bellow to show their territory and fight over females, sometimes hurting each other with their sharp antlers. Most of the time, one calf is born in the spring after.

Red deer live on moors (what we call swamps), mountainsides, and grassy areas close to forests. You can see them in parks with deer all over the U.K. Most of what Red Deer eat are grasses, sedges, rushes, and small bushes like heather, nettles, mint, and other herb plants.

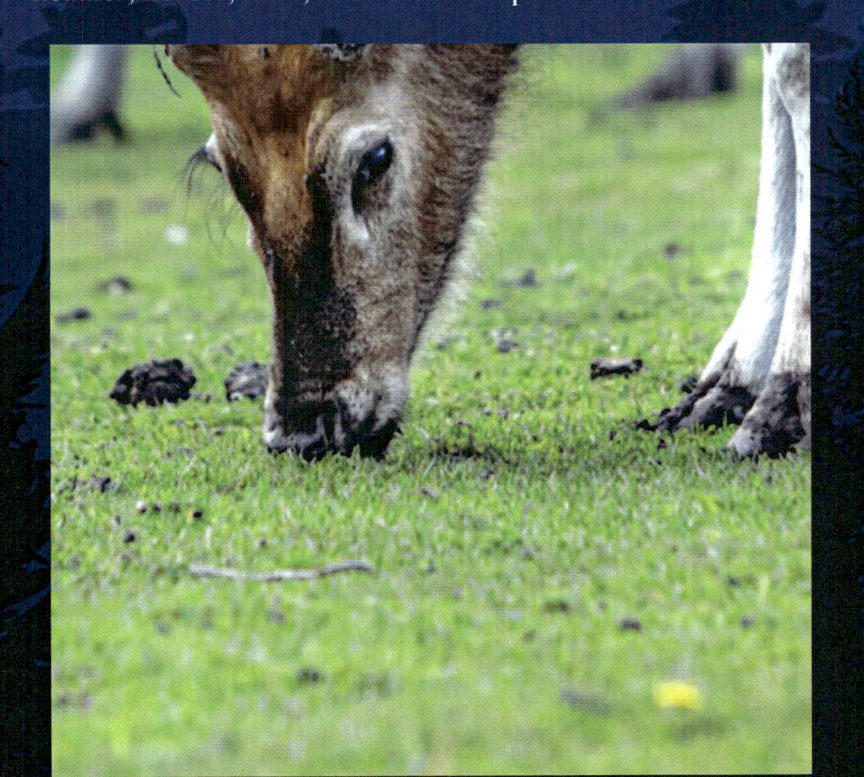

In the United States, like our ancestors before us, it is very easy to confuse seeing a Red Deer with seeing an Elk – they are very similar, with the only difference being that a Red Deer is a degree smaller than their Elk counterparts.

Knowing Your Gear

Getting a deer, Red Deer or not, without the right gear is almost impossible. It's important to have a gun or bow you can handle. Deer stands will also help you succeed, sure, but so will having good equipment. Good hunters take everything they need to kill a deer with them into the woods in one go.

Guns and Scopes

Most hunters use either a shotgun or a rifle for hunting deer, but there are other options that we'll cover too.

Shotguns

The 20-gauge and the 12-gauge are the most common types of shotguns used to hunt deer.

A 20-gauge is a good first gun for a young hunter. When fired, the kick, or recoil, is not as strong as with a 12-gauge, even though it sounds like it would be the other way around!

Shotguns can be loaded with either buckshot or slug shells, depending on the laws in your state. Be sure to know this ahead of time!

The difference is that buckshot shells are full of big pellets that spread out as they fly through the air like an old-fashioned B.B. gun. One big bullet comes out of a slug shell. Knowing this, it is easy to understand the difference between the two!

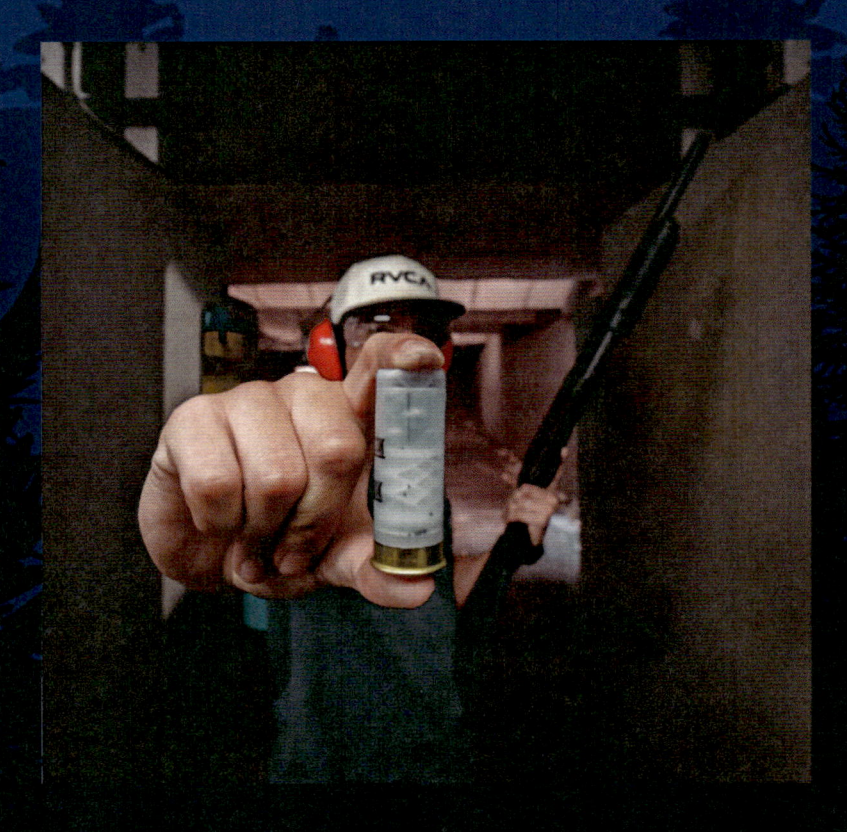

Rifles

If a hunter has a rifle, he or she can see farther through the scope – this is why many hunters like them. It can shoot one bullet that can hit a target hundreds of yards away. Because rifles are so strong, some states make it hard to use them for hunting deer because they are considered overpowered, considering how relatively harmless a deer is at a safe distance.

No matter what gun you choose, adding a scope can help you make the best shot. A 3 x 9 scope is the one most people use. This means that at its lowest setting, the scope magnifies the deer three times, and at its highest setting, it magnifies it nine times.

Scopes are helpful in the same way that using to reading small text with a magnifying glass is – they make it easier to land an accurate shot. While this is good for you as the hunter, it is also good for the deer, seeing as your shot has a higher potential of landing cleanly, meaning it will down the deer instantly rather than cause injury.

Arrows and Bows

Compound bows are what most bow hunters use. These bows have wires and cables that make it easy to pull the bowstring back, as compared to older bows and arrows like you've seen in history books that have a single bowstring.

Think about the draw weight when choosing a bow. This is the amount of pulling power you'll need to pull the arrow back and shoot it forward. Make sure you pick a weight that you can pull. You won't be able to shoot when you see a deer if you can't draw your bow, or it will just go a little way forward and fall to the ground.

Bowhunting Tips

- Most bowhunters who hunt deer use arrows with broadheads.
- Arrow shafts can be made of carbon or aluminum.
- Arrow shafts made of carbon are light and move quickly.
- The shafts of arrows made of aluminum are heavier and can go deeper into the deer but are a little bit heavier.

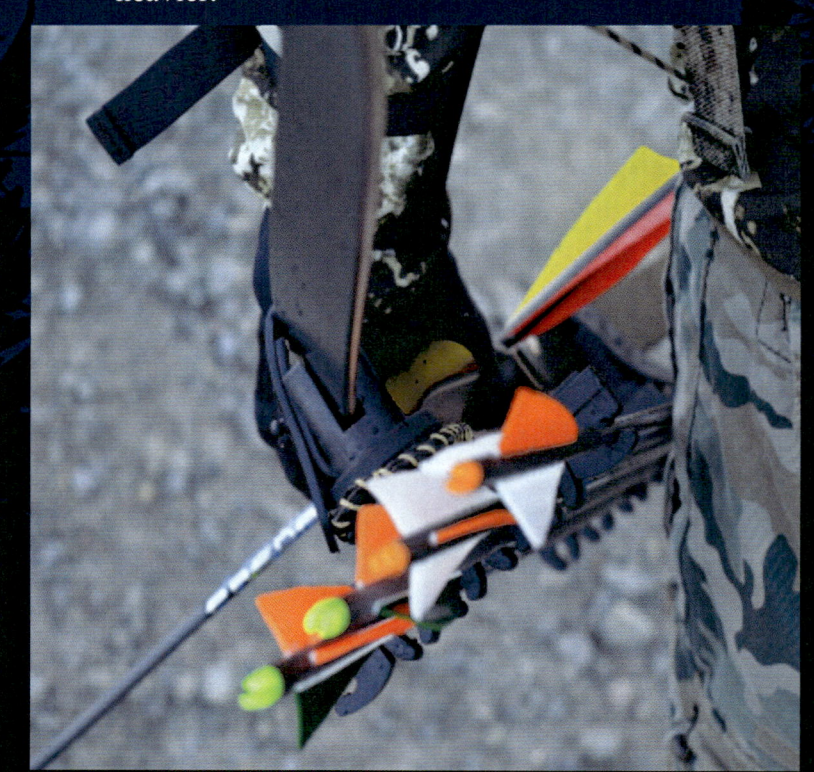

Safety

A big part of being safe with weapons is being aware of what's going on around you.

There are two huge, important things to remember:

1. Keep your gun or bow pointed in a safe direction, meaning not at anyone, and pay attention to who and what is around you.
2. Keep your gun's safety on at all times until you're ready to shoot. If you're hunting with a bow, keep your arrows in a quiver until you're ready to use them. If you trip and fall, the quiver will protect you from the sharp arrowheads.

Deer Stands

Many hunters hide in deer stands so that deer won't see them. You can get 10 to 20 feet off the ground with these stands. Some stands are just simple platforms with seats that are attached directly to the tree trunks and can even be carried around.

Some of the others are ladders and platforms that lean against trees or are attached to them. Some hunters even make their own deer stands that stand on their own so that they can come back to them year after year.

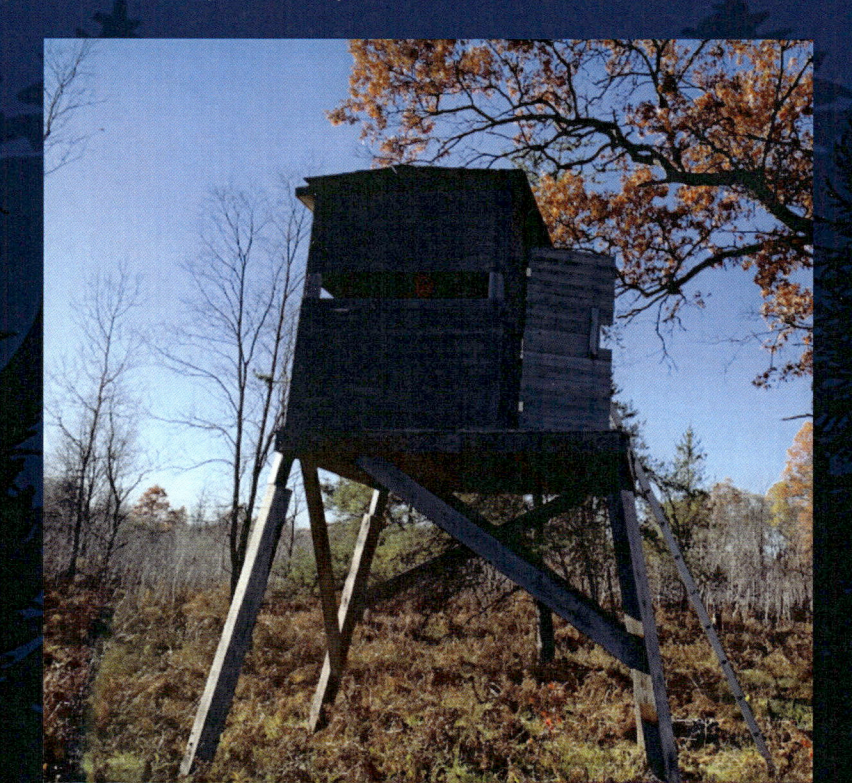

If you are going on a Red Deer hunt at an arranged facility, it is good to ask the owner or hunting party organizer if there are any permanent stands on the property and where they are or if you have permission to use lightweight do-it-yourself stands.

Deer Stand Safety

It is very important to stay safe as you climb and sit in your stand.

Don't try to bring your gun, bow, or arrows up with you to your deer stand. Instead, tie a rope around your unloaded gun and leave it on the ground. Once you are safely in your stand, use the rope to pull your weapon up to you. Also, make sure to wear a safety harness when you're sitting in your stand. If you lose your balance, a harness will keep you from going down.

This may sound silly, but these two tips could help to save your life if something goes wrong in your stand high up in the air.

Deer Scents

Even if you have the best gear, you won't shoot a deer that can smell you – they know to run away the moment they smell something strange in the air. Some hunters use skunk scent to cover up their smell – it isn't that deer will run from any smell; they run from really unfamiliar smells like human scents.

With just one or two drops of a scent cover, you can smell like anything but a person – and trick the deer. Skunks, foliage, dirt… There are a lot of smells out there. Hunters will give you plenty of opinions on what they think works best, but that choice is up to you to decide as you find your favorite.

Deer are also drawn to the smell of other deer, especially when it's time for them to mate. You can buy deer urine on the internet and in stores that sell hunting gear. With just a little bit of deer urine, you can get a deer to come to you. It is a smell they know and are attracted to, making the job of finding deer that much easier!

Scouting

Before you go hunting, you need to do some scouting to find the best spot, even at a hunting range or facility where deer are free to roam.

Use a field map if the facility provides one – while it won't necessarily tell you where to go straight to in order to find deer, it will show you where food and water sources are – safe to say they'll be close to that area.

Tracking

The better your chances of shooting a deer, the more work you put into scouting your area.

The first place to search for deer is on the ground. You can tell how big a deer is by looking at its tracks. For instance, a big, deep hoof print could mean that a big buck walked there. Female deer or young deer might have left tracks that were smaller and less deep. You can experiment with this tactic by watching footprints on the beach – fresh ones will be really well defined, but older ones will be worn down by the waves and gone within a minute or two.

The size of the tracks isn't the only way to tell how long ago the deer was in the area. Older tracks with soft, round edges have likely been worn down by rain and wind. The sharp edges of a deer's tracks show that it was just there. The newer the tracks, the more likely it is that you will see a deer in the area.

You can also track deer by looking for their laydown spots where foliage has been piled or disturbed, droppings, hair left behind, or antler rubs on trees where bucks mark their territory.

Aiming

Without a doubt, shooting a deer in the lungs is the quickest method to kill it – full-grown bucks have lungs the size of around a football and doe still have a large set as well, even if they are a bit smaller. As long as you aim for the lungs you will likely hit a critical area, since the heart is also close – aiming in this area also will keep you from missing or hurting the animal if it moves or jumps, which is likely, since your weapon will make some noise when fired.

Field Dressing

After you shoot a deer, it's time to clean it in the field. Field dressing is important because deer meat can go bad if it bleeds inside the body if you let it wait. Dressing your deer correctly in the field can save the meat by preventing bacteria from getting in to spoil it.

To get the organs out of a deer in the field, you'll need a knife and a game saw. Also, make sure you have disposable gloves to protect your hands, a cloth for cleaning up, and plastic bags for the organs. You can process the deer on the spot, bag up the meat, and take it home.

General Safety

Hunting deer is a fun sport, but it does come with some risks. When hunting in the field, it's important to follow a few safety rules.

1. Tell someone where you're going and how long you'll be gone before you leave. This, of course, is obvious if you're going to a hunting reserve.
2. Bring along a simple survival kit. Include a cell phone, water, a knife, first-aid supplies, rope, and a fire-starting kit that is waterproof.
3. Bring extra and wear safety equipment – most importantly, pieces the color blaze orange. This bright orange isn't visible to deer but is easily visible by other hunters.

And always ask an important question before you shoot: "Do I know for sure that it's a deer? "

It can be hard to tell the difference between a hunter and a deer from a distance. Because of this, most states require gun hunters to cover their clothes with blaze orange vests or jackets. Hunters can easily spot blaze orange. Most of the time, bowhunters don't have to wear blaze orange, unless they are hunting during gun season – still, it is a good idea to put some on anyway, since deer can't tell the difference.

Food to Pack

Unlike when fishing or other sports where sound isn't a problem, your food choices are a little more limited – after all, you don't want to eat anything that crunches, as you could possibly scare deer away! The big idea for taking food on a deer hunting trip is to pick foods that are easy to carry and easy to eat on the move.

Sandwiches

They are easy to store because they are oval or square and can fit in almost any box, pocket, or bag. Putting them in a plastic bag helps them stay fresh longer – not to mention you can eat them anywhere, just put down your weapon and eat!

Beef Jerky

Beef jerky is quiet and easy to eat with your hands, so you can eat it in a chair, blind, stand, boat, or even while standing – again, all you have to do is put your gear down for a second, eat, then move again. Also, beef jerky comes in handy pre-sealed containers and packets, so there's no worrying about littering or jerky going stale on the trail.

Soft Granola and Nutrition Bars

While snacks like chips and nuts that are crunchy will be a no-go because of the noise, granola and nutrition bars are an option since they are bound together and don't make a snapping noise when you eat them.

Understanding Conservation

Many people have a tradition of going deer hunting every year, and they look forward to it. But conservation groups and responsible hunters need to work together to keep this tradition going. Hunting is the act of a constant give and take.

The tradition of hunting deer is kept alive in large part by conservation groups. The group Whitetails Unlimited works to protect whitetail deer. Whitetails Unlimited was started in 1982. It raises money to teach people how to hunt, protect deer habitat, and study wildlife. In 1984, the Rocky Mountain Elk Foundation began working to protect and improve Elk habitats in North America. The group has helped bring back elk populations in the U.S. and Canada since it was started. These groups work to protect the environment for all wildlife, if they are raised on hunting ranges or not.

At the end of the day, being a good hunter is the best way to protect deer populations. Always let the place you hunt go back to how it was before, like you were never there. Deer usually stay away from places where hunters leave things behind. Throw away the empty shell casings and other trash. Remember, you are visiting the deer's home, not the other way around.

Recap

You bite your lip, double-checking your aim…

The deer moves a little, and you readjust…

You feel the pressure of your finger on the trigger…

You squeeze.

Your chances of success will be a series of factors leading up to this moment. Are you ready? Having read this book, you've already worked to increase your chances of success. You can do this.

Made in United States
North Haven, CT
01 February 2025